READING/WRITING COMPANION

Mc
Graw
Hill
Education

Cover: Nathan Love, Erwin Madrid

mheducation.com/prek-12

Send all inquiries to:
McGraw-Hill Education
Two Penn Plaza
New York, NY 10121

ISBN: 978-0-07-901792-5
MHID: 0-07-901792-4

Printed in the United States of America.

7 8 9 LMN 23 22 21   D

Welcome to Wonders!

Read exciting Literature, Science, and Social Studies texts!

★ LEARN about the world around you!

★ THINK, SPEAK, and WRITE about genres!

★ COLLABORATE in discussions and inquiry!

★ EXPRESS yourself!

my.mheducation.com

Use your student login to read texts and practice phonics, spelling, grammar, and more!

Unit 2 Our Community

The Big Idea

What makes a community?...8

Week 1 • Jobs Around Town

Talk About It...10

Shared Read "Good Job, Ben!" 12
Realistic Fiction...22
Character, Setting, Events 24

Anchor Text *The Red Hat*
Writing Respond to Reading 26
Analyze the Text 28

Paired Selection "Firefighters at Work"
Analyze the Text 31

Research and Inquiry.................................34
Make Connections.................................36

Digital Tools **Find this eBook and other resources at:** my.mheducation.com

Week 2 • Buildings All Around

Talk About It..**38**

Shared Read "Cubs in a Hut"...........................**40**

Fantasy...**50**

Character, Setting, Events **52**

Anchor Text *The Pigs, the Wolf, and the Mud*

Writing Respond to Reading **54**

Analyze the Text **56**

Paired Selection "Homes Around the World"

Analyze the Text **59**

Research and Inquiry **62**

Make Connections.......................................**64**

Week 3 • A Community in Nature

Talk About It...**66**

Shared Read "The Best Spot".....................................**68**

Nonfiction **78**

Main Topic and Key Details **80**

Anchor Text *At a Pond*

Writing Respond to Reading.................................**82**

Analyze the Text **84**

Paired Selection "Way Down Deep"

Analyze the Text **87**

Research and Inquiry...**90**

Make Connections...**92**

Week 4 • Let's Help

Talk About It..94

Shared Read "Thump Thump Helps Out"...................96

Fantasy..106

Character, Setting, Events...........................108

Anchor Text *Nell's Books*

Writing **Respond to Reading**........................110

Analyze the Text.....................................112

Paired Selection "Kids Can Help!"

Analyze the Text.....................................115

Research and Inquiry.................................118

Make Connections....................................120

Week 5 • Follow the Map

Talk About It..122

Shared Read "Which Way on the Map?"....................124

Nonfiction 134

Main Topic and Key Details.......................................136

Anchor Text *Fun with Maps*

Writing **Respond to Reading** 138

Analyze the Text 140

Paired Selection "North, East, South, or West?"

Analyze the Text 142

Research and Inquiry...144

Make Connections..146

Writing and Grammar

Fantasy

Analyze the Student Model 148
Plan 150
Draft 152
Revise and Edit 154
Share and Evaluate/Publish 156

Wrap Up the Unit

Show What You Learned

Realistic Fiction: "Where Is Rex?" 158
Nonfiction: "Jobs, Jobs, Jobs" 161

Extend Your Learning

Focus on Poetry 164
Respond to the Read Aloud 166
Expand Vocabulary: Direction Words 168
Connect to Content 170

Writing Friendly Letter 172
Choose Your Own Book 174

Track Your Progress

What Did You Learn? 175

Our Community

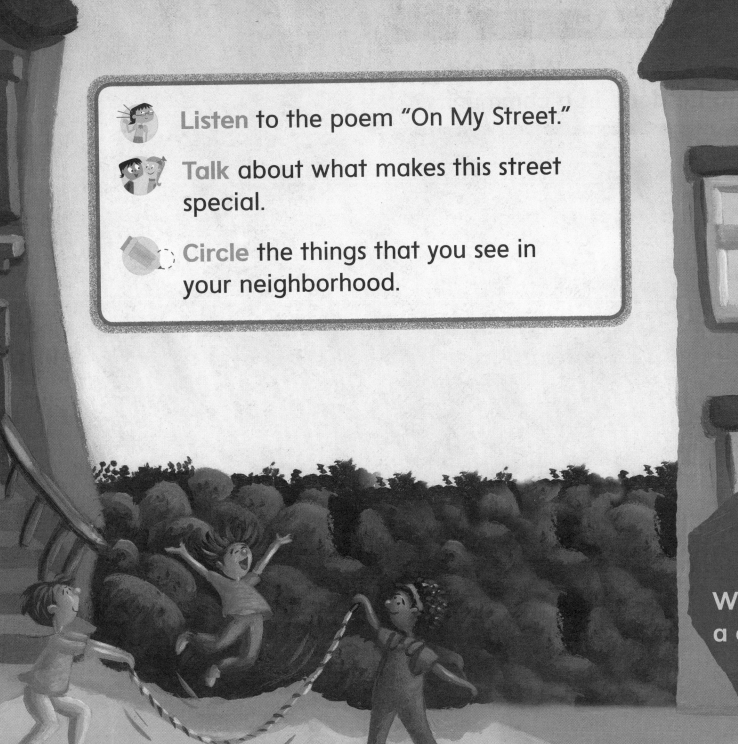

Listen to the poem "On My Street."

Talk about what makes this street special.

Circle the things that you see in your neighborhood.

The Big Idea

What makes a community?

Talk About It

Essential Question What jobs need to be done in a community?

Talk about why this man's job is important for a community.

 Write about other jobs you know.

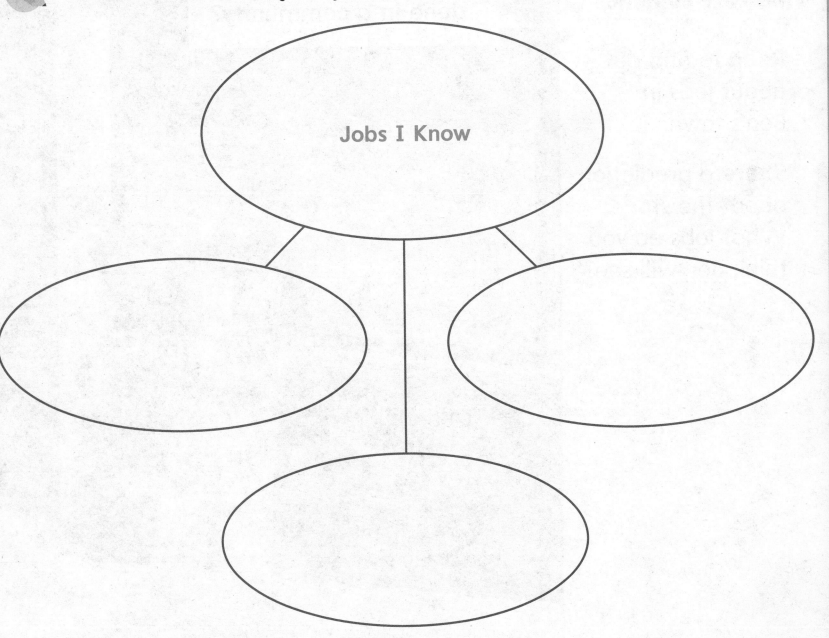

Jobs I Know

Shared Read

 Find Text Evidence

What jobs need to be done in a community?

 Read to find out about jobs in Ben's town.

 Share a prediction about the story. What jobs do you think Ben will see?

Good Job, Ben!

Realistic Fiction

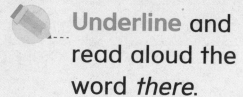 **Find Text Evidence**

Underline and read aloud the word *there*.

Circle and read aloud each word with the short *e* sound as in *bed*.

Ben and Mom head to town.
It is a big trip.
There is a lot to see.

Ben and Mom will get on the bus.
The driver stops on this block.

Good job!

Find Text Evidence

 Underline and read aloud the words *help, use, new* and *again.*

 Talk about who helps Mom and Ben cross. How does she help?

Ben and Mom can not cross yet. Stop! Stop! She can help.

Big job!

Ben and Mom can walk.
Six men use a drill and fill cracks.
It will look new again.

Wet job!

Find Text Evidence

 Talk about who helps Jet.

 Think about your prediction. Are these jobs that you see in your town?

Ben and Mom step in for bread. Ben sniffs. It smells good. Yum! Mom gets ten.

Hot job!

Ben and Mom get Jet.
Jet licks Ben.
The vet helped Jet get well quick.

Pet job!

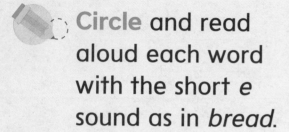

Find Text Evidence

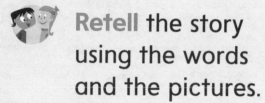 **Circle** and read aloud each word with the short *e* sound as in *bread*.

Retell the story using the words and the pictures.

Ben and Mom stop to get books.
Ben can get help from Miss Glenn.

Glad job!

What did Ben get?
What has he read?
Ben read books on jobs.

Good job, Ben!

Remember, realistic fiction is a genre. It is a made-up story. It has characters that do things that could happen in real life.

 Reread to find out what makes this story realistic fiction.

 Share how you know it is realistic fiction.

 Write about the characters. Then write something they do that could happen in real life.

Who Could Be Real?	What Could Really Happen?
1.	1.
2.	2.

Characters are the people or animals in a story. To understand the characters, think about what they say and do. The **setting** is where the story takes place. The **events** are what happens in the story.

 Reread "Good Job, Ben!"

 Talk about the characters, setting, and events on pages 14-15.

 Describe the characters, setting, and events in the story. Write these details on the chart.

Character	Setting	Events

Retell the story in your own words.

Write about the story.

Why did Jen get wet?

_____

- -

_____

- -

_____

Text Evidence

Page

How does Jen help Jim?

_____

- -

_____

- -

_____

Text Evidence

Page

Anchor Text

 Talk about how the stories are the same and different.

 Write about the stories.

How is Jen's job like the jobs in Ben's community?

_____

- -

_____

- -

_____

Which job do you like best?

_____

- -

_____

- -

_____

Quick Tip

Use the pictures to think about which job you would like to do.

Jobs Around Town **27**

Talk about what Jen is doing on pages 10–13.

Write clues from the story that answer the questions.

What wakes Jen up?	What does she do next?

Why is it important for Jen to move fast?

_____

- -

_____

- -

_____

Talk about what Jen does on pages 15–17.

 Write about what Jen does after the bell rings again.

What does Jen do?

How does the author show that Jen is brave?

_____

- -

_____

_____

- -

_____

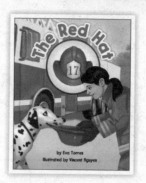

 Talk about who says "thank you" to Jen on page 19.

 Write clues from the pictures that help complete the chart.

What Jen Does	How Jim feels

Why does Jim say "thank you" to Jen?

_____

_____

_____

 Write About It

Would you like to have Jen's job? Tell what you would like or not like, and why.

Firefighters at Work

A bell rings at the firehouse. Firefighters slide down a pole. They put on special clothes.

boots

hat

jacket

Read to find out what firefighters do.

Talk about what firefighters wear in the photo. Circle the labels.

Underline clues that tell what firefighters do when the bell rings.

Fuse/Getty Images

The brave firefighters get to work. They use hoses to spray water. Their special clothes protect them. They put out the fire!

Underline the words that tell what the special clothes do.

Circle the word that tells what is used to spray water.

Talk about why firefighters are brave. Use evidence from the text.

Quick Tip

Photos show what firefighters do that makes them brave.

Talk about what you learn about firefighters from the photos.

 Write clues that tell the important things firefighters do. Use the text and photos.

The text tells me...	The photos show me...

How does the author help you learn what firefighters do?

_____

- -

_____

- -

_____

Talk About It

How does the author show that firefighters have an important job?

This text tells that firefighters . . .

Jobs in the Community

Step 1 **Pick** a person you know to interview.

What is their job?

_____

- -

_____

Step 2 **Write** three questions that you want to ask.
Find out why their job is important.

_____

- -

_____

- -

_____

- -

_____

Step 3 Interview the person. Write the answers you received.

_____
- -
_____
- -
_____
- -
_____

Step 4 Think about your interview. Why is this job important for a community?

_____
- -
_____

Step 5 Choose how to present your work.

Talk about what the people in the painting are doing.

 Compare how this job and Jen's job are similar.

Quick Tip

You can talk about this painting using these sentence starters:

These people help others by . . .

Jen helps others by . . .

These people are cutting wheat, an important food crop.

What I Know Now

Think about the texts you heard and read this week about jobs. Write what you learned.

_____

_____

_____

_____

 Think about other jobs you want to learn about. Tell your partner.

 Share one thing you learned about realistic fiction.

Talk About It

? Essential Question What buildings do you know? What are they made of?

Talk about the buildings in this city.

Write what you think the buildings are made of.

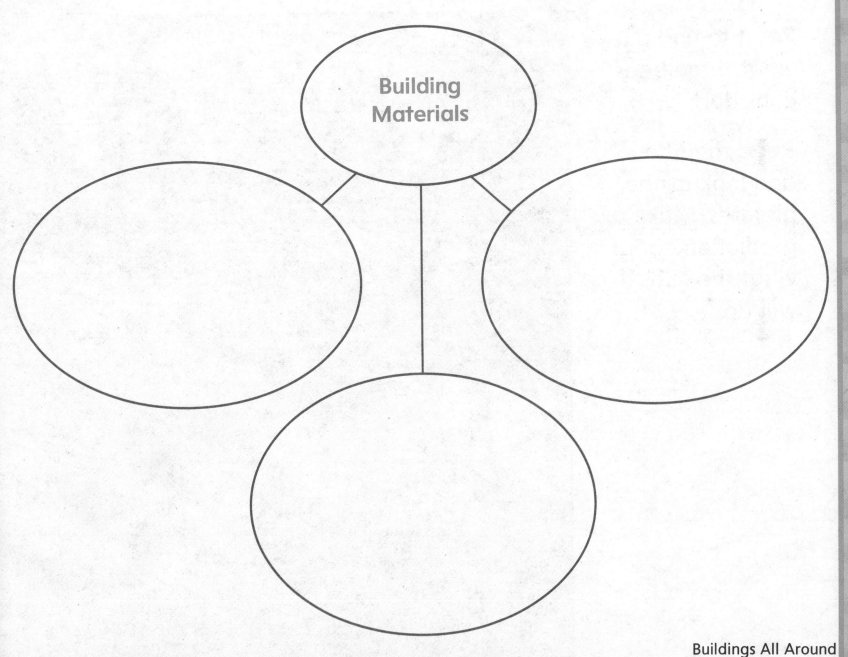

Building Materials

Shared Read

Find Text Evidence

Read to find out what three bear cubs do.

Read the title and look at the pictures. Make a prediction about what the cubs will do.

What buildings do you know? What are they made of?

Cubs in a Hut

Find Text Evidence

 Underline and read aloud the word *could*.

Look at the pictures. Talk about your prediction. Was it correct? Do you need to change it?

"Let's make a hut," said Gus.

"We could use mud," said Russ.

"It will be fun!" said Bud.

The cubs had a plan.
Bud got a big stack of sticks.
Russ and Gus got mud
and grass.

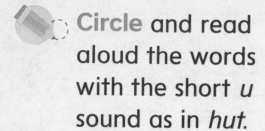

Find Text Evidence

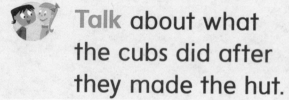
Circle and read aloud the words with the short *u* sound as in *hut*.

Talk about what the cubs did after they made the hut.

The cubs did a very good job.

"Let's move in!" yelled Russ.

"Yes, yes!" yelled Bud and Gus.

The cubs set up rugs and beds.
They filled up the hut with lots
of stuff.

Find Text Evidence

 Underline and read aloud the words *then, one, three,* and *live.*

Talk about the cubs' problem. Why are they wet?

Then one night three cubs got up.

Drip, drip, drip!

"My bed is wet!" yelled Bud.

"My head is wet!" yelled Gus.

"It's not fun to live in a wet hut!" yelled Russ.

Shared Read

 Find Text Evidence

Circle and read aloud the words with the short *u* sound as in *hut*.

Retell the story using the pictures and words.

"We must fix it," said Bud.

"It will not drip on us," said Gus.

"We will not get wet," said Russ.

It is good to live in a dry hut.
Three cubs are as snug as bugs
in a rug!

Remember, a **fantasy** is a made-up story. It often has characters that could not exist in real life. It can have a problem and solution.

 Reread to find out what makes this story a fantasy.

 Share how you know it is a fantasy.

 Write two problems the characters have. Tell how they find a solution.

What is the problem?	What is the solution?
1.	1.
2.	2.

Remember, **characters** are the people or animals in a story. The **setting** is where the story takes place. The **events** are what happen in the story. Think about what the characters do and say and what happens to them so you can describe events.

 Reread "Cubs in a Hut."

 Talk about the characters, setting, and events.

 Describe the characters, setting, and events. Write these details on the chart.

Characters	Setting	Events

Respond to the Anchor Text

Retell the story in your own words.

Write about the story.

The Pigs, the Wolf, and the Mud
by Ellen Tarlow
Illustrated by Pablo Bernasconi

Why can't the wolf blow down the pigs' hut?

_____

- - - - - - - - - - - - - - - - - - - -

_____

- - - - - - - - - - - - - - - - - - - -

_____

Text Evidence

Page

Why doesn't the wolf eat the pigs?

- - - - - - - - - - - - - - - - - - - -

_____

- - - - - - - - - - - - - - - - - - - -

_____

Text Evidence

Page

Talk about how the stories are the same and different.

Write about the stories.

How are the cubs and the pigs alike?

_____

_____

_____

How do the houses in each story keep the characters safe?

_____

_____

_____

Make Inferences

Use details to figure out things that are not stated.

The wolf does not like mud. How do the pigs use the mud to stay safe?

Talk about pages 28–29. Tell about the pigs and their home.

 Write clues from the story that answer the questions.

What is the pigs' home like?	How do the pigs feel about their home?

Why is the mud hut a good place for the pigs to live?

_____

_____

_____

Talk about what the wolf thinks of mud on pages 33–34.

 Write clues from the text and pictures that tell you how the wolf feels.

What does the wolf do?	How does the wolf feel about mud?

Why is the mud hut a bad place for the wolf to try to eat the pigs?

_____

- -

_____

- -

_____

Talk about the pigs' plan to build a new hut on page 41.

Write clues that help you know who likes the plan and who does not.

Who likes it?	Who does not?

Why is a new mud hut a good idea?

_____

- -

_____

- -

_____

 Write About It

Write directions for the pigs to follow when building their hut.

Homes Around the World

This is a good home for a wet place. There is a lot of water here. The stilts help keep this home dry.

This home is made of wood.

 Read to find out why these are good homes.

 Underline the word that tells what the home is made of.

 Talk about places where you might find a home like this.

James Strachan/robertharding/Getty Images

There is a lot of ice in this place. People can use it to build. This is an igloo. People don't live in igloos. But they are good shelter from the cold.

An igloo is made of ice.

Vova Shevchuk/Shutterstock.com

Underline the word that tells what the igloo is made of.

Circle the word that tells what people do with the ice.

Talk about why this is a good shelter for a cold and windy place.

Quick Tip

Use the captions to understand what you see in the photos.

Talk about what makes each home on pages 59 and 60 special.

 Write your answers.

Why is the home on page 59 a good home for a wet place?	
Why is the home on page 60 a good home for a cold place?	

Why is "Homes Around the World" is a good title?

_____

_____

_____

_____

Talk About It

How does the author show that homes are often built to fit their environment?

Research and Inquiry

Research a Building

Step 1 **Pick** a type of building to write about.

_____

- -

_____

Step 2 **Decide** what you want to know about your building. Write your questions.

_____

- -

_____

_____

- -

_____

_____

- -

_____

Step 3 **Decide** where to find the information you need. Read for answers to your questions.

Step 4 Write what you learned about your building.

_____

- - - - - - - - - - - - - - - - - - -

_____

- - - - - - - - - - - - - - - - - - -

_____

- - - - - - - - - - - - - - - - - - -

_____

- - - - - - - - - - - - - - - - - - -

_____

- - - - - - - - - - - - - - - - - - -

_____

- - - - - - - - - - - - - - - - - - -

_____

Step 5 Draw your building. Use labels to give information about your building.

Step 6 Choose how to present your work.

Talk about what this house is made of.

Compare how this house is different from the house of the three pigs.

Arpad Benedek/E+/Getty Images

This home is made of recycled bottles.

Quick Tip

You can use the captions to talk about this photo using these sentence starters:

This house has . . .

The three pigs' house is made of . . .

What I Know Now

Think about the texts you heard and read this week about buildings. Write what you learned.

_____

- -

_____

_____

- -

_____

_____

- -

_____

 Think about other buildings you want to learn about. Share your ideas with a partner.

 Share one thing you learned this week about fantasy stories.

Talk About It

Essential Question **Where** do animals live together?

Talk about where these penguins live.

Write about a penguin's habitat.

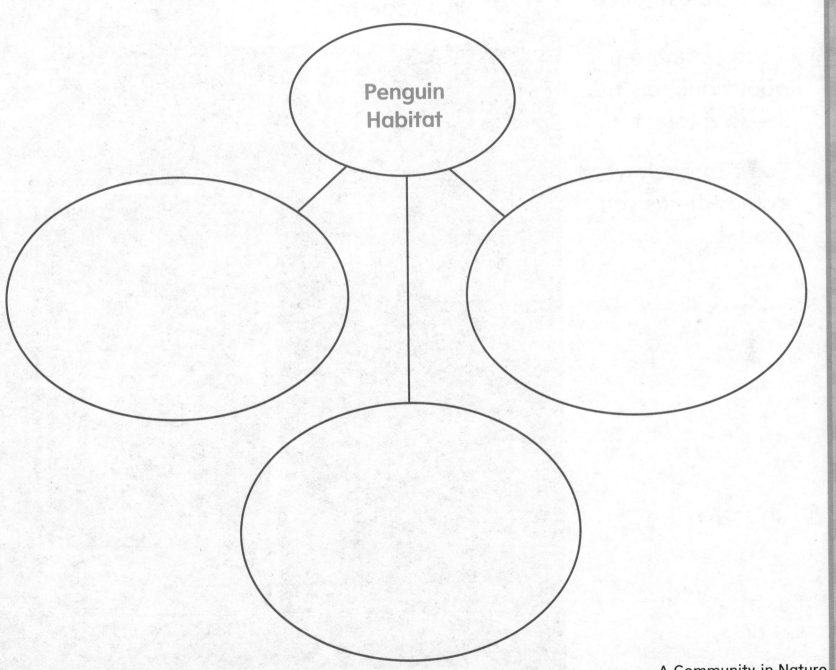

Penguin Habitat

Peter Scoones/The Image Bank/Getty Images

Find Text Evidence

 Read to find out about animals that live in a forest.

Point to each word in the title as you read it.

(bkgd) AVTG/Vetta/Getty Images; (inset) Theo Allofs/Corbis Documentary/Getty Images

Essential Question

? Where do animals live together?

The Best Spot

Shared Read

 Find Text Evidence

 Underline and read aloud the words *of*, *eat*, and *who*.

Circle the text that tells what deer eat.

This is a forest.

This spot has lots of animals.

Deer live here. They eat plants.

Purestock/Getty Images; (border) Carl Keyes/Alamy

But who is in the grass?

A rabbit's head pops up!

Find Text Evidence

Think about the animals that live in nests. Reread and use the photos if you are not sure.

Circle the word with the same ending sounds as in *sunk*.

What is up there?

Look up, up, up.

It is a nest.

The mom gets big bugs. Yum!

What is on the trunk?

It is a nest, too.

Lots of wasps live in it.

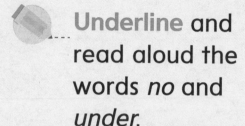

Find Text Evidence

Underline and read aloud the words *no* and *under*.

Circle the words with the same ending sounds as in *land*.

Ants live here, too.

Ants pick up twigs and grass.

Ants zip in and out.

Ants have no rest!

Way In

Food

Ant Digging

Queen Ant

Eggs

Ants dig under sand and grass.

Shared Read

 Talk about what kits are. Reread the text and use the photos if you are not sure.

Retell the text using pictures and words.

Fox kits hop on a stump.

Mom fox lets the kits run and jump.

The kits must eat.

Dad fox hunts at dusk.

tbkmedia.de/Alamy; (border) Carl Keyes/Alamy

Who went hunting, too?
A skunk!

This spot has lots of animals!

Remember, nonfiction is a genre. A nonfiction text gives facts and can be organized by description.

 Reread "The Best Spot" to find out how the text is organized.

 Share what part of the forest rabbits live in.

 Write the names of animals and the part of the forest where they live.

Animal	Part of the Forest Where It Lives
1.	1.
2.	2.
3.	3.

The main topic is what the text is about. Key details tell information about the main topic.

 Reread "The Best Spot."

 Talk about the main topic and key details in the text.

 Write the main topic and key details about animals that live in the forest.

Main Topic

Detail	Detail	Detail

Respond to the Anchor Text

 Retell the text in your own words.

 Write about the text.

Why is the pond a good place for frogs to live?

_____

- -

_____

- -

_____

Text Evidence

Page

Why do ducks go to the pond?

_____

- -

_____

- -

_____

Text Evidence

Page

 Talk about how the texts are the same and different.

 Write about the texts.

How are the texts alike?

_____

- -

_____

- -

_____

How is each place good for the animals that live there?

_____

- -

_____

- -

_____

Make Inferences

Think about how the animals in each habitat get their food.

The pond provides....

The forest provides....

Talk about the questions on pages 50–51.

Write clues from pages 52–55 to complete the chart. Use the photos to help you.

Who is under the water?	Who can fly to the pond?

Why does the author ask questions at the beginning of the text?

_____

- -

_____

- -

_____

Talk about the question the author asks on page 55.

 Write clues from the text and photos that answer the question.

What Text Says	What Photos Show

Who is in the eggs?

_____

- -

_____

- -

_____

Talk about how the turtles and fish are different on pages 56–57.

Write clues that come from the text and photos.

Turtles	Fish

What does the author want to show on pages 56–57?

_____

- -

_____

- -

_____

 Write About It

Write two more pages about one of the animals in *At a Pond*. Use the photos to help you.

"Way Down Deep"

 Talk about the words that repeat. What do they tell you?

 Write the words that repeat.

Why does the author repeat words in the poem?

Quick Tip

You can find clues in the text that help you know what the poem is about.

Talk about the third line of the poem. Say the words aloud to a partner. Alliteration in a poem is when two or more nearby words have the same beginning sound.

 Write the three words that have the same beginning sound.

Why does the author use the same sound in these words? Share your answer.

Talk about the words that tell how the animals move in the poem.

 Write clues that tell how the animals move.

How do the animals move?

What do the words tell you about the bottom of the sea?

_____

- - - - - - - - - - - - - - - - - - - -

_____

- - - - - - - - - - - - - - - - - - - -

_____

Talk About It

How does the author show what the bottom of the sea is like?

This author uses . . .

Where Animals Live

Step 1 **Pick** an animal. Think about where it lives.

Step 2 **Decide** where to find the information on its habitat.

_____

- -

_____

Step 3 **Read** about the animal. Write what you learned.

_____

- -

_____

- -

_____

Step 4 Draw the animal you learned about.
Use labels to show its environment.

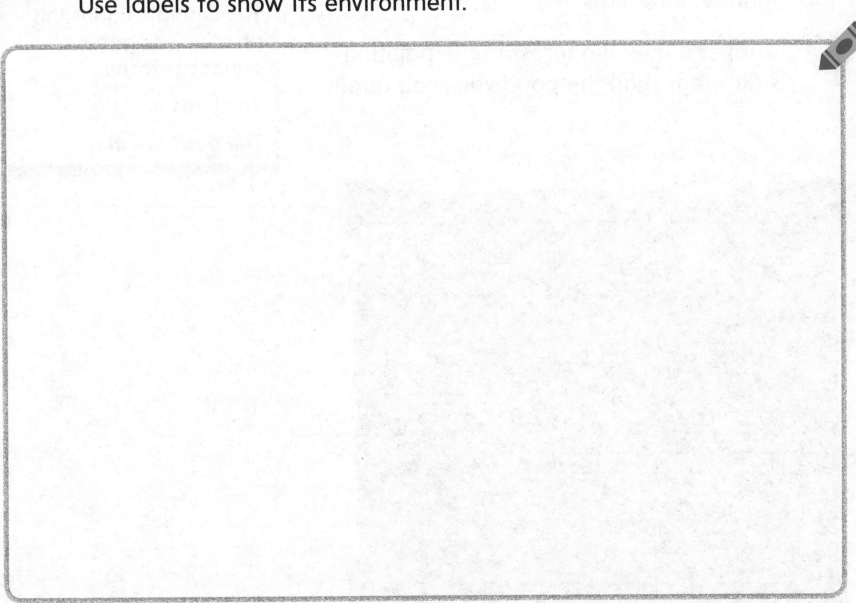

Step 5 Choose how to present your work.

Talk about what the painting shows about where birds live.

 Compare how the forest in the painting is different than the pond you read about.

Yale University Art Gallery

Birds build a nest high in a tree.

What I Know Now

Think about the texts you heard and read this week about where animals live. Write what you learned.

_____

_____

_____

_____

_____

_____

_____

 Think about other places animals live. Which places would you like to learn more about?

 Share one thing you learned this week about nonfiction.

Talk About It

Essential Question How do people help out in the community?

Talk about what these kids are doing.

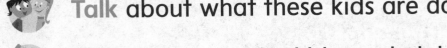

Write the ways the kids are helping their community.

How a Community Garden Helps

Read

Shared Read

 Find Text Evidence

 Read to find out how one rabbit helps his community.

 Circle and read aloud the words with the same beginning sound as *think*.

Essential Question

? **How do people help out in the community?**

Thump Thump Helps Out

Underline and read aloud the word *all*.

Think about what you read. Reread and look at the pictures if you do not understand something.

Thump Thump liked to thump.

He thumped a lot as he sang.

He thumped a lot just for fun.

"Hush! Stop that, Thump Thump!" yelled all the little rabbits.

"We do not like it one bit!"

But Thump Thump did not stop.

Shared Read

 Talk about why the big rabbits do not help the little rabbits.

Underline and read aloud the words *day*, *her*, and *call*.

One day, there was a problem.

Thump Thump's bus hit a rock.

Bang! Crash! Clunk!

His bus got stuck in the mud.

The little rabbits could not fix it.

"We wish big rabbits could get us home," sniffed the little rabbits.

"Help us!" yelled Miss Sheldon.

But not one big rabbit heard her call.

Shared Read

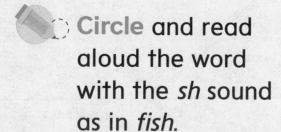 **Circle** and read aloud the word with the *sh* sound as in *fish*.

Think about what you read. Reread and use the pictures if you do not understand something.

Thump Thump had a plan.

"I think I can help," he sang.

He thumped and thumped and thumped.

Big rabbits all overheard
Thump Thump's thump.

They rushed to help fix the bus.

The kids got home fast.

Shared Read

 Find Text Evidence

 Circle and read aloud words with the *ng* sound as in *ring*.

Retell the text using the pictures and words from the story.

"Thump Thump, can you help us?" asked the big rabbits.

"We want you to thump loud and long if a rabbit needs help."

"Thump, Thump!" went Thump Thump, with a song.

And Thump Thump thumps and brings help to this day.

Remember, **fantasy** is a genre. It is a made-up story. It can have characters that do not exist in real life.

 Reread "Thump Thump Helps Out" to find out what makes it a fantasy story.

 Share how you know it is a fantasy story.

 Write two things Thump Thump does that show this is a fantasy story.

What Happens	Why It Could Not Happen In Real Life
I.	I.
2.	2.

Remember, **characters** are the people or animals in a story. The **setting** is where the story takes place. The **events** are what happens in the story. Describing what the characters say and do, the setting, and events will help you understand the story.

 Reread "Thump Thump Helps Out."

 Talk about the characters, setting, and events on pages 98–99.

 Describe the characters, setting, and events. Write these details on the chart.

Characters	Setting	Events

Respond to the Anchor Text

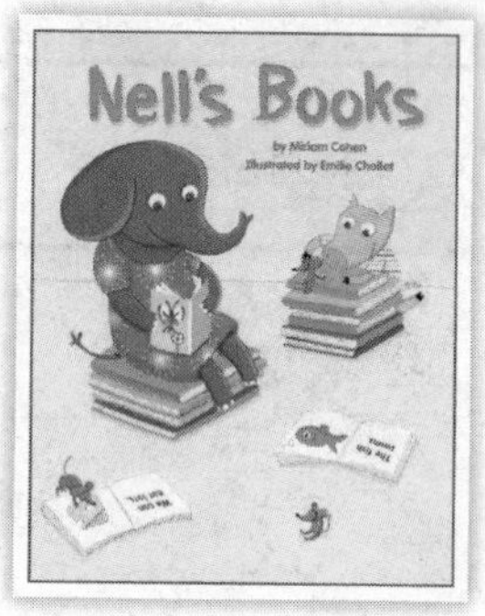

Retell the story in your own words.

Write about the story.

Why doesn't Nell want to play with Cat or Dog?

Text Evidence

Page

Why do the friends get a truck with books for Nell?

Text Evidence

Page

 Talk about how the stories are alike and different.

 Write about the stories.

How are Thump Thump and Nell alike?

_____

_____

_____

What important lesson do both texts teach?

_____

_____

_____

 Combine Information

As you read each page, think about how your ideas about Nell change.

Anchor Text

 Talk about what Nell is doing on pages 66–67.

Write clues from the story and pictures that help you know this.

I know that Nell . . .	I found a clue in the . . .

How do you know Nell likes to read a lot?

_____

- -

_____

- -

_____

Talk about how Nell's friends feel about reading on pages 72–75.

 Write clues from the pictures that help you answer the question.

Clues from pages 72–73	Clues from pages 74–75

How do the pictures help you know her friends' feelings about reading change?

_____

- -

_____

_____

 Talk about what Nell's friends say on pages 76–77.

Write clues to complete the chart.

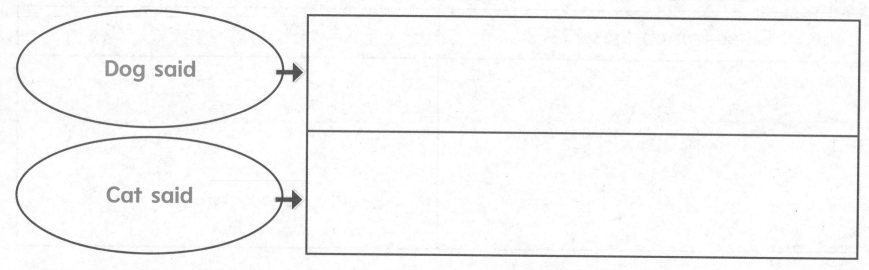

Dog said →

Cat said →

How does the dialogue help you know why Nell's friends got her a truck?

_____

- - - - - - - - - - - - - - - - - - -

_____

- - - - - - - - - - - - - - - - - - -

_____

 Write About It

Use *Nell's Books* as a model to write a fantasy about a character who helps.

Kids Can Help!

How can kids help the neighborhood? Kids can help grow a garden! It is fun to plant seeds and help them grow.

Underline the words that tell what kids can do to help the neighborhood.

Talk about how these kids help their community.

Kids can help clean the playground. They can pick up trash. They can recycle cans and bottles.

Recycling makes the neighborhood clean. Recycling helps our Earth, too.

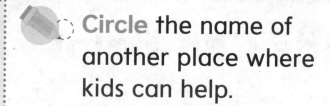 **Circle** the name of another place where kids can help.

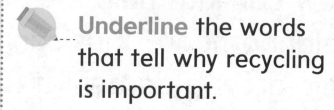 **Underline** the words that tell why recycling is important.

Talk about what the boys in the photo are doing.

Ariel Skelley/Blend Images/Getty Images

Quick Tip

You can use the photo to figure out what recycling means.

The photo shows . . .

Recycling means . . .

Talk about the question the author asks on page 115.

Write clues from the text and photos about how kids can help.

In the garden	At the playground

Why is "Kids Can Help!" a good title for this text?

_____

- -

_____

_____

- -

_____

Talk About It

How does the author show that kids can help?

Classroom Helpers

Step 1 **Pick** a classmate to interview.

_____

- -

_____

Step 2 **Write** two questions to ask your classmate about how he or she helps in the classroom.

_____

- -

_____

- -

_____

_____

- -

_____

_____

- -

_____

Step 3 Write what you learned about your classmate.

_____

\- -

_____

\- -

_____

Step 4 Draw how your classmate helps in the classroom.

Step 5 Choose how to present your work.

Talk about what Little Boy Blue's job is.

 Compare how Thump Thump and Little Boy Blue are alike.

Little Boy Blue

Little boy blue, come blow your horn;

The sheep's in the meadow,

The cow's in the corn.

Where is the boy who looks after the sheep?

He's under the haystack, fast asleep.

Quick Tip

You can compare both characters with these sentence starters:

Thump Thump helps by . . .

Little Boy Blue helps by . . .

What I Know Now

Think about the texts you heard and read this week about how people help in their community. Write what you learned.

_____

- -

_____

- -

_____

- -

_____

 Think about what else you want to learn about helping others. Tell your partner.

 Share one thing you learned about fantasy stories.

Talk About It

Essential Question How can you find your way around?

Talk about what this family is doing.
What does this map show?

 Write about when you might need
to use a map.

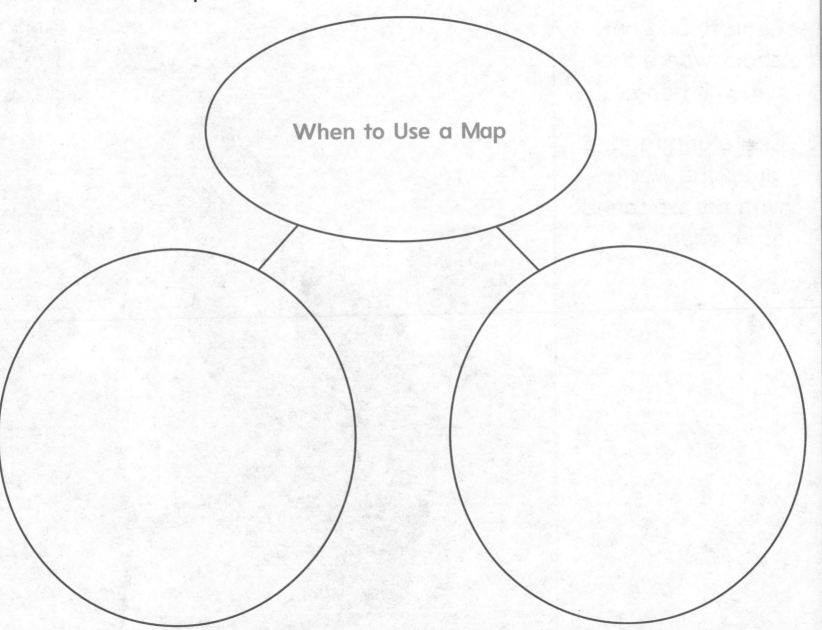

When to Use a Map

Shared Read

 Find Text Evidence

 Read to find out about where the two children go.

 Circle and read aloud the words with the *wh* sound as in *when*.

Essential Question

? How can you find your way around?

Which Way on the Map?

Find Text Evidence

 Underline and read aloud the words *walk*, *around*, and *place*.

Think about what you read. Reread and use the pictures if you do not understand something.

Mitch and Steph live in a big town.

There is a lot to see.

Let's walk around with them.

This is the town on a map.

It shows each place in town.

Shared Read

Find Text Evidence

Circle and read aloud the word with the same *tch* sound as *catch*.

Talk about the school on the map. Tell what is near it.

This place has red bricks.

Many children go here.

Mitch and Steph go here, too.

Which place is this?

Can you spot it on the map?

Shared Read

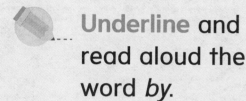

✏️ Underline and read aloud the word *by*.

💭 Think about what you read. Reread and use the photos if you do not understand something.

This place is by a lake. People chat on benches. Mitch and Steph will run and play catch.

It is such fun!

Which place is this?

Can you spot it on the map?

Shared Read

Find Text Evidence

 Talk about the post office. What do people do there?

 Retell the text using the pictures and words.

This place has a big box. Mitch and Steph stop and get stamps.

They drop a letter in the big box.

Which place is this?

Can you spot it on the map?

Where can Mitch and
Steph get lunch?

Check the map!

Remember, **nonfiction** is a genre. A nonfiction text gives facts about real places. It can use maps to give information.

 Reread to find out what makes this a nonfiction text.

 Share how you know it is nonfiction.

 Write facts about the maps on pages 127, 129 and 131.

Map	What the Map Shows
Page 127	
Page 129	
Page 131	

Remember, the main topic is what the text is about. Key details give information about the main topic.

 Reread "Which Way on the Map?"

 Talk about the main topic. What do you learn from Mitch and Steph?

 Write about the main topic and key details.

Main Topic

Detail

Detail

Detail

Retell the text in your own words.

Write about the text.

Which map shows the names of streets?

Text Evidence

Page

_____

- -

_____

- -

_____

Which maps use a key?

Text Evidence

Page

_____

- -

_____

_____

- -

_____

Talk about how the texts are the same and different.

 Write about the texts.

Which map in "Fun with Maps" is most similar to the map Mitch and Steph use?

_____

_____

_____

Which map do you think you might like to use? Tell why.

_____

_____

_____

Quick Tip

What kind of map did Mitch and Steph use?

Mitch and Steph used a map of a . . .

Their map is similar to the map of . . .

Talk about the titles of the maps on pages 87–89.

 Write clues from the text and pictures that tell what you see in each map.

Phil's room	Town of Chatwell

What kinds of places does that the author create maps for?

_____

- -

_____

- -

_____

Talk about the map key on page 91.

 Write three clues from the key that name the places on the map.

What does the map key show?

How does the map key help you understand the map?

_____

- -

_____

- -

_____

 Write About It

Why does the author show different kinds of maps? What does this help us understand about maps?

"North, East, South, or West?"

Many maps show directions. North, East, South, and West are directions. Directions tell us which way to go.

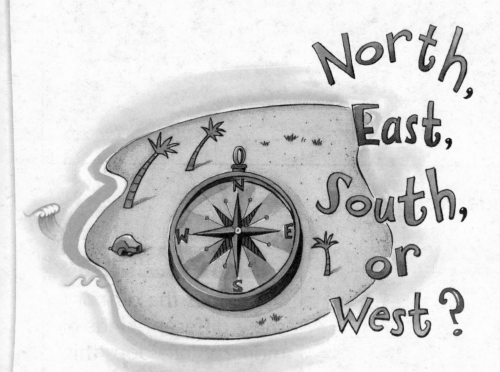

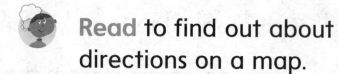

Read to find out about directions on a map.

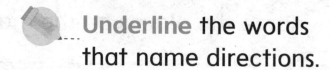

Underline the words that name directions.

Circle the letters N, E, S, and W in the picture of the compass.

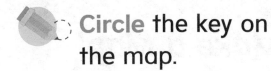
Circle the key on the map.

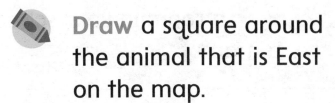
Draw a square around the animal that is East on the map.

Talk about how the key on the map can help you.

Talk About It

Talk about how this text can help people.

Let's Make a Map!

Step 1 **Pick** a room in your school to create a map of.

_____

- -

_____

Step 2 **List** the things in your room to include in your map.

_____

- -

_____

- -

_____

- -

_____

Step 3 Draw a map of the room with things in the correct place. Add a title and key.

Step 4 Choose how to present your work.

Talk about what the dots in the map show. Use the caption to help you.

 Compare how this map is similar to the maps you read about.

In this star map, the dots show where stars are located. Words tell the names of groups of stars.

What I Know Now

Think about the texts you heard and read this week about maps. Write what you learned.

_____

- -

_____

- -

_____

- -

_____

- -

_____

 Think about what else you want to learn about maps. Tell your partner.

 Share one thing you learned about nonfiction.

Writing and Grammar

Alex

I wrote a fantasy story. My story has characters that could not be real.

Fantasy

My fantasy story has events that could not happen in real life.

Student Model

Betty's Hats

Betty is a very busy octopus.

She lives in the sea.

She likes to knit hats for her friends.

She likes to use different colors.

She works fast!

Genre

 Talk about what makes Alex's story a fantasy.

 Ask any questions you have.

 Circle something that could not happen in real life.

Plan

 Talk about characters for a fantasy story.

 Draw or **write** about the characters and what they do.

Quick Tip

Think about characters and events that could not happen in real life.

Choose a fantasy character to write about.

_____

- -

_____

- -

_____

Tell what your character does.

_____

- -

_____

- -

_____

- -

_____

 Circle what makes your story a fantasy.

Writing and Grammar

Draft

Read Alex's draft of his fantasy story.

Character, Setting, Events

My story has a character, setting and events.

Student Model

Betty's Hats

Betty is a very busy octopus.

She lives in the sea.

She likes to knit hats.

She likes to use colors.

She works very fast!

Ideas

I included descriptive details.

Revise and Edit

Think about how Alex revised and edited his fantasy story.

Student Model

I used a proper noun correctly.

Betty's Hats

Betty is a very busy octopus.

She lives in the sea.

She likes to knit hats for her friends.

I added details to make my writing more interesting.

- A noun names a person, place, or thing. It can be common or proper.

- A singular noun names one thing. A plural noun names many things.

I added details to make my writing more clear.

I used an exclamation mark at the end of my exclamation.

She likes to use different colors.

She works fast!

I added details to my drawing.

Your Turn

Revise and edit your writing in your writer's notebook. Use your checklist. Be sure to use nouns correctly. Check your punctuation.

Publish

 Finish editing your writing. Make sure it is neat and ready to publish.

 Practice presenting your work with a partner. Use this checklist.

 Present your work.

Review Your Work	Yes	No
Writing		
I wrote a fantasy story.	☐	☐
I used descriptive details.	☐	☐
Speaking and Listening		
I spoke clearly.	☐	☐
I listened carefully to others.	☐	☐
I asked questions to get information.	☐	☐

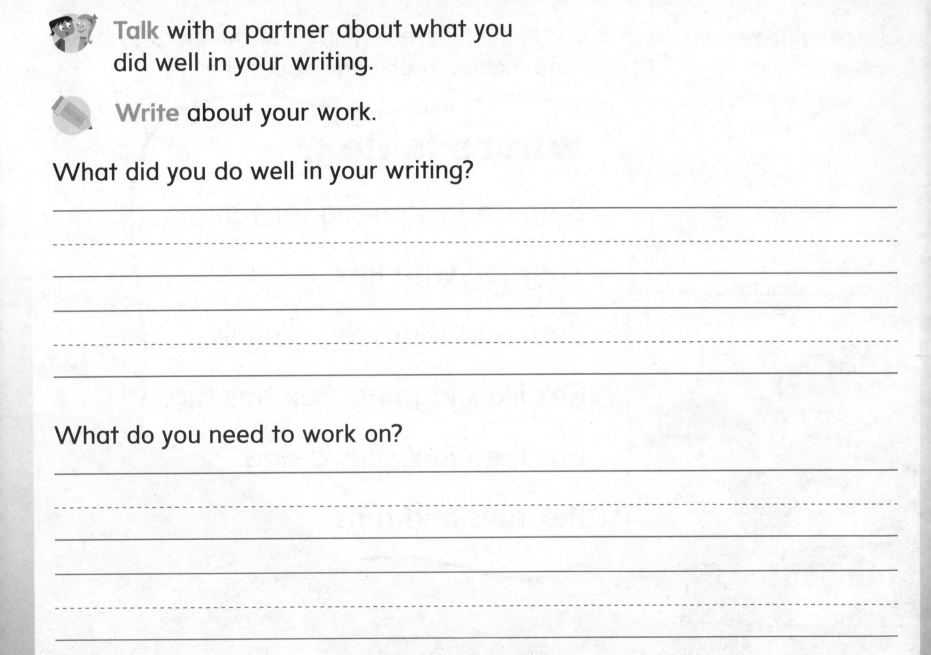

Talk with a partner about what you did well in your writing.

Write about your work.

What did you do well in your writing?

_____

- -

_____

- -

_____

What do you need to work on?

_____

- -

_____

- -

_____

Show What You Learned

Spiral Review

Genre:
- Realistic Fiction
- Nonfiction

Strategy:
- Make and Confirm Predictions, Reread

Skill:
- Character, Setting, Events; Main Topic and Key Details

 Read "Where Is Rex?" Use the pictures to make a prediction about the story.

Where Is Rex?

Beth and Mom jog for fun.

They jog with Rex.

Beth and Mom jog up hills.

Rex likes jogging. Rex has fun.

But then Rex sees a dog.

Rex runs and runs.

"Come back, Rex!" calls Beth.

Beth and Mom run fast.

Beth looks and looks.

Is Rex lost? Rex is not lost.

Rex is with his pal, Ted.

That Rex!

Ted

Show What You Learned

Circle the correct answer to each question.

1 How can you tell the story is realistic fiction?

A The story tells facts about running.
B Dogs can talk.
C People and dogs can run in real life.

2 Where do Beth and Mom like to jog?

A They jog at home.
B They jog up hills.
C They jog in a park.

3 Why does Rex run and run?

A He sees a dog.
B He is lost.
C He is hungry.

> **Quick Tip**
>
> Talk about the characters, setting and events in the story.
>
> Rex runs because . . .
>
> Rex is . . .

Read "Jobs, Jobs, Jobs."

 Reread the text if you do not understand something. Use the photos to help you.

Jobs, Jobs, Jobs

Jobs, job, jobs.

There are lots of jobs.

You can be a vet. Vets make pets well.

This vet checks a dog's head.

Vets can make sick dogs, cats, and fish well.

Jobs, job, jobs.

Look at this job.

This man plants many crops.

This man can plant yams.

This man can plant plums.

This man checks the crops.

The crops get big.

Jobs, jobs, jobs.

Circle the correct answer to each question.

1 How do you know this is nonfiction text?

   A It uses characters that could not happen in real life.

   B It gives facts about real people.

   C It tells a made-up story.

2 What is the main topic of this text?

   A jobs

   B cars

   C plants

3 What is this man's job?

   A He drives a bus.

   B He checks pets.

   C He plants crops.

Quick Tip

Look at the photos when you reread text to help you answer the question.

Focus on Poetry

Poetry is a genre. A poem is a kind of writing that has short lines. It often has rhyme. It may also have repetition, or words that repeat.

 Listen to "Way Down Deep."

 Talk about the words that repeat. What do they tell you about the bottom of the ocean?

Write two more lines to the poem.
Use words that repeat.

_____

- -

_____

- -

_____

- -

_____

- -

_____

 Share why you chose to repeat the words
that you did.

Respond to the Read Aloud

The **events** are what happens in the beginning, middle, and end of a story.

 Listen to "Finn's Perfect Job."

 Talk about what happens in the story.

 Write about three of the main events.

1.

2.

3.

Extend Your Learning

Expand Vocabulary

You learned direction words in this unit: North, South, East, and West.

 Talk about when to use direction words.

 Write the direction words on each compass point.

 Say each direction word aloud. Point to each word as you say it.

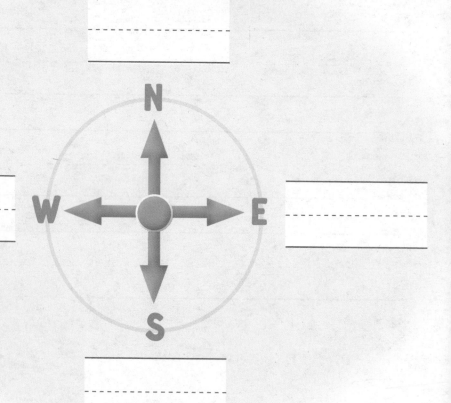

Some other direction words are left, right, up, and down.

 Look at the map. Use direction words to tell what you see.

Animal Communities

Find out more about animal habitats.
Choose an animal to research.

 Talk about questions you have about where the animal lives.

 Write your questions in your writer's notebook. Then use books or the Internet to find the answers.

 Share your answers and information with the class.

W. Perry Conway/age fotostock

Reading Digitally

Online texts sometimes have links you can click on. Listen to "Help Your Community" at my.mheducation.com.

 Talk about what happens when you click the first link.

 Write about the last link. What information does it give you?

_____

_____

_____

_____

Write a Friendly Letter

You can share news with a friend by writing a friendly letter.

 Look and listen to this friendly letter.

The **greeting** tells who the letter is for.

Write your news in the **body** of the letter.

The **closing** tells who the letter is from.

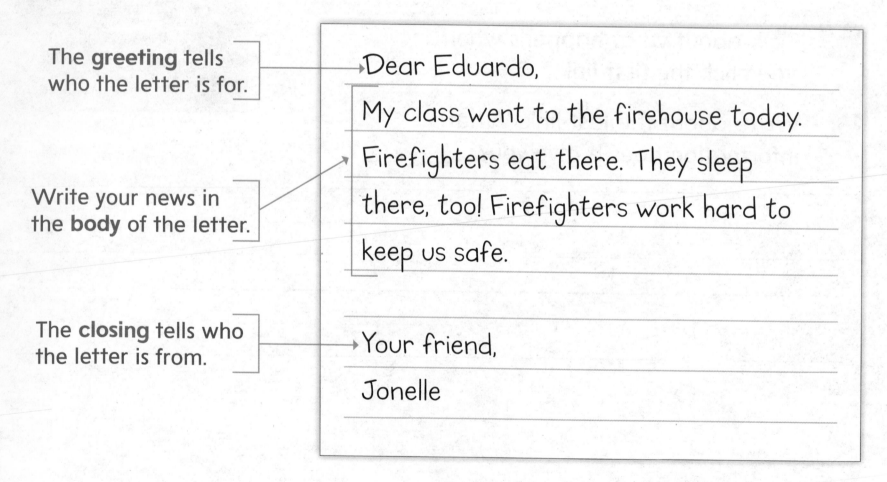

Dear Eduardo,

My class went to the firehouse today. Firefighters eat there. They sleep there, too! Firefighters work hard to keep us safe.

Your friend,

Jonelle

Talk about a friendly letter you would like to write.

 Write your friendly letter.

Dear _____,

From,

Choose Your Own Book

 Tell a partner about a book you want to read. Say why you want to read it.

Write the title.

_____

- -

_____

Write what you liked about the book.

Minutes I Read

_____

- -

_____

- -

_____

- -

_____

What Did You Learn?

Think about the skills you learned.
How happy are you with what you can do?

I understand character, setting, and events.	🙂	😐	🙁
I understand the main topic and key details.	🙂	😐	🙁

What is something that you want to get better at?

_____

_____

_____

My Sound-Spellings

Aa apple
a

Bb bat
b

Cc camel
c ck k

Dd dolphin
d
_ed

Ee egg
e
ea

Ff fire
f
ph

Gg guitar
g

Hh hippo
h_

Ii insect
i

Jj jump
j dge
ge gi_

Kk koala
c k ck

Ll lemon
l
_le

Mm map
m

Nn nest
n
kn_ gn

Oo octopus
o

Pp piano
p

Qq queen
qu_

Rr rose
r
wr_

Ss sun
s
ce ci_

Tt turtle
t
_ed

Uu umbrella
u

Vv volcano
v

Ww window
w_

Xx box
x

Yy yo-yo
y_

Zz zipper
z
_s

th	sh	ch tch	wh_	ng	a ai_ _ay a_e ea ei	i y i_e igh ie
thumb	shell	cheese	whale	sing	train	five

o 'oa ow o_e _oe	u u_e _ew _ue	e_e ea ee e _y ie _ey	ar	er ir ur or	oar or ore	ow ou
boat	cube	tree	star	shirt	corn	cow

oi _oy	oo	oo u_e u _ew ue ou ui	a aw au augh al	air are ear ere
boy	book	spoon	straw	chair

Aa Bb Cc Dd Ee

Ff Gg Hh Ii Jj

Kk Ll Mm Nn

Oo Pp Qq Rr

Ss Tt Uu Vv

Ww Xx Yy Zz